THE ROYAL HORTICULTURAL SOCIETY
PRACTICAL GUIDE

ARCHES
& PERGOLAS

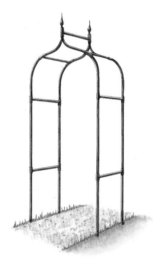

THE ROYAL HORTICULTURAL SOCIETY
PRACTICAL GUIDES

ARCHES
& PERGOLAS

RICHARD KEY

DORLING KINDERSLEY
LONDON • NEW YORK • SYDNEY
www.dk.com

A DORLING KINDERSLEY BOOK
www.dk.com

PROJECT EDITOR Lesley Malkin
ART EDITOR Wendy Bartlet

SERIES EDITOR Gillian Roberts
SERIES ART EDITOR Stephen Josland

SENIOR MANAGING EDITOR Mary-Clare Jerram
MANAGING ART EDITOR Lee Griffiths

DTP DESIGNER Louise Paddick

PRODUCTION Mandy Inness

First published in Great Britain in 2000
by Dorling Kindersley Limited,
9 Henrietta Street, London WC2E 8PS

A CIP catalogue record for this book is available from the British Library.
ISBN 0 7513 0758 0

Reproduced by Colourscan, Singapore
Printed and bound by Star Standard Industries, Singapore

CONTENTS

USING ARCHES AND PERGOLAS

TRADITIONAL USES

Pergolas and arches have long been used successfully in garden design to provide strong vertical elements. Their purpose has usually been twofold: to frame views and openings, and to provide welcome shade over areas set aside for entertaining and relaxation. Covered by, and supporting, climbing plants, pergolas can form cool retreats in shaded walkways and arbours.

FRAMING ENTRANCES
Since before the Middle Ages, archways in many styles have been constructed to form grand entrances. Initially, arches in garden settings were built from brick or wrought iron, and would be in place to highlight an opening in a garden wall or form a simple link between two areas within the garden. At the time of the Renaissance, archways came to be positioned to frame a view or other focal point of interest. Then, as now, the impact of the distant, or partially hidden, view was far stronger. It was not until the last century that the arch itself was framed with shrubs and climbing plants.

STRUCTURES FOR SHADE
A pergola may be thought of as a series of arches linked together to form a simple framework, most usually constructed from timber posts and beams, and intended to support climbing plants.

◄ ARCH ENTRANCE
This fifteenth-century illumination of a garden scene shows an archway with side trellis panels, its purpose simply to form a link between two adjacent areas within the garden.

◄ SHADED ARBOUR *Statuary and pots enhance a cool, secluded walkway.*

The original pergola constructions can be traced back to ancient Egyptian times, when overhead structures were used as a support for vines, which in turn provided much-needed areas of shade. These pergolas, often constructed with stone pillars for strength, were built throughout the hot regions of the Middle East. From here, their use spread to more temperate climates, where their function became more ornamental. They still had, in part, the role of providing shade but, in these cooler regions where total shade was not required, care needed to be taken in the design of pergolas, as sturdy structures with close-set beams could appear oppressive and gloomy. Thus in time the horizontal beams were spaced further apart to let in more light. Rounded poles were often used as cross-beams because they shed water more effectively than square sawn timber, which holds water on its flat surface.

COVERED WALKWAYS

Today, arbours may be viewed primarily as a focal point. Often enclosed on three sides, they tend to be smaller than pergolas, and are usually set in a cool corner of the

GRAND VERANDA
Original pergolas with stone pillars and overhead timber beams were used to support vines and provide shade. Here, a stately pergola of similar construction, supports a beautiful wisteria to create a cool colonnade on the sunny side of this imposing house.

◀ ARBOUR RETREAT
A white bench on a small area of paving draws the eye to this private place where a canopy of beams and trailing climbers, including hop and jasmine, provide welcome shade, and peaceful seclusion in which to rest.

▼ ROSE-COVERED ARCH
An old-fashioned rose-covered arch, here with rambler 'Dorothy Perkins', looks wonderful in a country garden. The black picket gate looks just right framing the opening to the vegetable garden beyond.

garden. Originally, however, arbours were shady tunnels formed by training trees, such as linden and plane, to grow over a framework of metal arches. The long, cool, dark tunnels would give a sense of mystery, eventually leading on to a bright and open

The original arbours were trees trained to grow over metal arches

space. Traditional arbours were linear, although similar shaded walkways were sometimes led around an inner courtyard in the style of a cloister garden. Arbours were also developed as secluded outdoor rooms, shaded places often enclosed by intricate trellis work. This is more in line with their function today, where trees, climbers, and shrubs are trained over wooden archways and trellis to form a secluded haven.

CONTEMPORARY USES

TODAY'S ARCHES AND PERGOLAS are closely linked to earlier constructions, but other than to provide shade, their function tends to be purely ornamental. Grape vines are still grown over these structures, as are other climbers, also chosen for their fragrance and colour. Traditional structures remain desirable in many settings, although the cost and time to build is a major commitment.

ARCHES AS SIGHT LINES

Although arches maintain their traditional use over an entrance or an opening, their far more important function in contemporary design has become to frame a view, or to form an opening into another part of the garden. Arches are now most often built as free-standing "viewing panels" or windows through which to catch glimpses of other areas within the garden. This technique has been used successfully with timber frame archways, sometimes further enhanced with trellis and even stained glass panels, offering both clear views and tinted images.

MODERN ARBOURS

These days the term arbour applies to the construction of a shaded alcove offering a cool retreat. Arbours are usually formed

▲ USING STAINED GLASS
A hop-covered timber framework, with stained glass set into it, gives interesting images, and is an effective way of screening unwanted views.

▼ ARBOUR WITH SWING SEAT
Pots of pelargoniums and the scent of lilies further enhance the setting of this triangular arbour, with its unusual suspended swing seat.

from a pergola construction, with either slatted timber or trellis on three sides.

Manufacturers of garden structures have been quick to take up the popular trend for nostalgia so you may find that even contemporary arbours are modelled on old designs; Victorian, for example. Many are grand affairs, sited to command a view over the garden and surrounding area, or set as a focal point to attract the eye and

> Build arches as viewing panels through which to glimpse the garden

form a welcome shaded seat.

On a more modest scale, other arbours are available as post-and-rail construction kits with bolt-on trellis panels, which may be planted up, added to, or adapted to screen functional utility areas, neighbouring windows and even the street.

MODERN PERGOLA
With its open, lightweight metal beams, this striking modern pergola is more a feature in itself than a practical shade-casting structure. It suits its cool-climate garden where deep shade is not essential.

SHADED COVER OVER TERRACES

Whether a freestanding construction or a "lean-to" with overhead beams attached to a house wall, the main use of the pergola today is to provide shaded cover over a terrace for alfresco entertaining. Overhead beams alongside the house – especially when clothed in climbing plants – help keep adjacent living rooms cool in summer, protect furnishings from the fading effect of strong sunlight, and form a good visual link between the house and garden. This association is successful because the open canopy of overhead beams and climbers becomes an effective transition between the solid roof of the house and the foliage and branch structure of the surrounding vegetation.

CONTRASTING
SHAPES
*This cleverly designed
modern pergola uses
contrasting shapes to
add to its impact. The
unusually tall red
posts are balanced by
equally elongated
overhanging beams,
which link well with
the softer shapes of
interlocking circles in
the side panels.*

In many ways, a pergola with overhead beams is more satisfactory than a structure with either a solid canopy or a glass roof. A solid roof can run the risk of providing too much shade and appearing too heavy; it casts no interesting patterns of light and shadow and allows little air circulation. Glass roofs, while letting in more light, may become too hot and cause glare, requiring some form of screening and so again casting too much shade. A roof such as this will, of course, protect you from rain but the noise in a storm may prove too loud for you to remain comfortable anyway.

Modern pergolas are really no more than a new look at a very old type of structure,

designed to be inexpensive and easy to build. The do-it-yourself pergola kits currently available come with pre-notched cross-beams and posts, corner braces (often prefixed with waterproof glue), and planed posts with a bevelled edge, all made from timber guaranteed against rot.

The use of today's structures has spread to encompass more contemporary functions such as carports: a timber framework with a roof of slatted timber and climbing plants is far more attractive than utilitarian corrugated plastic roofing. This slatted timber construction has also been used to good effect in the building of shadehouses, which allow you to grow shade-loving plants in gardens with no natural shade.

Pergolas have really taken over from traditional arbours as shaded walkways, even in small gardens. The traditional Italianate theme of a cloister-like shaded walkway around a central, open courtyard can be very successful today in small town gardens. Here, a walkway around the garden can have the effect of making the space feel bigger – and that the overhead beams offer some privacy from surrounding

> Today's pergolas are no more than a new look at an old type of structure

tall buildings is a bonus. Modern pergolas offer a new look at shading sitting areas, too. Indeed, some pergolas offer a far stronger statement than one of pure function and practicality. Overhead beams in minimalist schemes or posts in painted steel or timber become arresting focal points; the intricate pattern of light and shade may even be their sole purpose.

▲ BOLD COLOUR
A red pergola walkway highlights the vogue for oriental-style gardens, reinforced here by a planting that includes maples and bamboos.

▼ WEB OF BLUE
This striking blue pergola needs no vegetation at all, as the web of shadow patterns cast by the overhead beams creates its own interest.

Design Considerations

Vertical interest is an important element in any garden, especially one with no existing mature trees. This is where arches and pergolas come into their own as they offer instant height, which can be softened quickly by fast-growing climbers. Do take care, however, that there is a strong purpose for the inclusion of such a feature, whether to frame or hide a view, or to provide welcome shade.

Division and Screening

A pergola, linked with panels of trellis or slatted timber if you wish, can provide a successful physical and visual barrier from one part of the garden to another. This may be an ideal way to screen the vegetable garden, sheds, or utility areas.

Well-positioned archways are good for access, but avoid a central arch in a narrow garden as this tends to split the garden down the middle and draw the eye through to the rear boundary. In this case, site the opening to one side of the garden and lead a path across to it. This will give greater movement in the garden and prevent a straight view from one end to the other. Carefully sited pergolas can also obscure unsightly views beyond the garden, while

DIVISION
Sturdy brick piers and the closely spaced crisscross of beams overhead combine to form a secluded and shaded seating area. The side panels and plants in raised beds create a neat division from other parts of the garden, adding to the feeling of comfort and privacy.

overhead beams may offer privacy from neighbouring windows, so providing greater comfort when sitting outdoors.

SIMPLICITY AND SCALE

The construction of arches and pergolas should be bold and strong: where possible, avoid flimsy arches, which will collapse under the weight of mature climbers or, at best, take on a drunken gait. Simple timber post-and-beam constructions usually work best, with little need for elaborate detail unless you are aiming to match an existing structure. Although new structures may look stark and heavy initially, they will be softened in time as climbing plants mature.

Try to suit the scale of your structure to the size of your house and garden. For example, a large pergola with stone pillars and massive oak beams will almost certainly look out of place in the garden of a small terraced house.

PRINCIPLES TO FOLLOW

- Avoid central arches in narrow gardens.
- Pergolas of simple design and strong construction are best.
- Arbours and arches make good focal points, but one is enough in a small garden.
- Introduce movement with walkways, which should always lead somewhere.
- Enclose arches on either side to maintain the mystery of the space beyond.
- Use overhead beams to help create privacy from neighbouring windows.
- Treat flimsy structures as temporary features.
- Ensure the scale of the structure is in keeping with its surroundings.

ARCH IN PERFECT SCALE
The rounded "window" of this rose-covered arch is simply and perfectly proportioned. Painted white, it complements the cool greens and creamy-whites of the nearby planting.

SHADED SEAT
This is a wonderful example of an arbour acting as a focal point. The white-painted woodwork, pitched roof with finials, and rambling roses certainly draw the eye but the side trellis panels and tall planting ensure that the arbour sits comfortably within the overall design of the garden.

Movement and Focal Points

A garden with movement allows you to experience it from different views and perspectives, offering maximum enjoyment of the whole. Arches and pergolas can help to introduce a sense of movement around even small gardens. An archway will allow access, inviting you to walk from one area to another, while a pergola over a pathway leads you on to another part of the garden.

All gardens should include at least one area for relaxation; aside from its primary function as somewhere to sit, it is itself a place of interest and reason for movement. Plan a lean-to or freestanding pergola to provide shade and screening over a sitting area, or build an arbour in the cool shade of overhanging tree branches.

Focal points are important to attract attention and give visual movement within a garden, but take care not to have too many as this can look fussy and be tiring on the eye. Arches are obvious points of focus and are often used to good effect in leading the eye to the front gate or other access points, for example, thus giving clear

> ## Use arches to give visual movement and attract attention

directions to visitors. Arbours, too, are often seen as focal points, enticing you to a cool seat on a hot day. The effect is far more appealing, however, if the arbour is softened and half-hidden by plants growing nearby, rather than placed squarely in the middle of a lawn.

MYSTERY AND TENSION

Tree tunnels in centuries past were designed to create a feeling of mystery and tension. Today's shaded pergola walks aim to do the same, fostering a sense of intrigue as you pass through the dappled half-light formed by overhead beams and climbers. The longer the walk, the greater the underlying sense of tension, which is broken only when you emerge, inevitably, into full light.

On a long pergola run it is a good idea to create a break – an arch or open doorway – possibly with a bench on which to rest and look out into the garden. These pauses themselves form tension points, creating a tantalizing sense of imminent discovery, inviting you into the open space beyond.

It is essential that the planting is linked, too. At ground level, plants disguise the posts and fill the gaps, while bare beams standing alone, with none of the nearby space hidden, mean that all sense of mystery is lost.

▲ STONE URN
A statue or other focal point such as this stone urn at the end of a pergola walkway can foreshorten the view, but it attracts attention, and will help to create a sense of movement.

◀ MYSTERY
A rose-covered metal arch fosters a delicious sense of intrigue: more of the garden appears to lie tantalizingly out of sight to the left and right of the lily-filled tub. Note how the black-painted arch mimics the colour of the rose stems.

STYLE AND MATERIALS

IN GENERAL, ARCHES AND PERGOLAS should look at home in their surroundings. Just as the size and scale of your construction should be in proportion to that of the house and garden, so their given style should be in keeping, too. The style of a structure owes much to the material from which it is made, although very different effects can be achieved using the same materials.

INFLUENCES ON STYLE

While rigid rules about the style of arches and pergolas are inappropriate, one main guideline can be followed: traditional constructions tend to be ideal in gardens of period homes, while more up-to-date structures are suited to modern dwellings.

That said, there is – as with sculpture – a wonderful sense of surprise in discovering a striking, contemporary work of art in the grounds of a country manor. This planned juxtaposition of styles can apply to arches, pergolas, and arbours, too, although it is only really practical to introduce mixes of style into larger gardens.

SUGGESTED MATERIALS

- **Country garden:** Oak (or other hardwood) pergola or brick piers with oak beams.
- **Coastal garden:** Reclaimed oak beams or driftwood for a traditional garden. Planed, stained timber for a contemporary feel.
- **Roof garden:** Strained galvanized wires for overhead climbers or a light plastic pergola.
- **Riverside garden:** Pergola made from machine-rounded wooden poles.
- **Mountain garden:** Pillars built from rubble walling, with rough-hewn timber beams.
- **Formal classical garden:** Smooth stone columns with planed, shaped timber beams.
- **Town garden:** Brick pillars, smooth beams.

TRADITIONAL
PERGOLA
There is movement here, but no great sense of urgency, and an almost timeless quality about this traditional pergola. A bench is placed for rest after a gentle stroll past lavender bushes under old oak beams, silvered with age, and climbing roses supported by natural stone piers.

The now truly cosmopolitan aspect of garden design allows you to link the style of a pergola to that of the garden. Books, television programmes, and international garden shows have ensured a burgeoning of eclectic garden styles. Anything goes. In a Mediterranean-style garden, for example, a pergola might have clean, uncluttered lines of bright-coloured timber; a country garden may have a rustic oak pergola or brick pillars with oak beams, whereas a modern, town roof garden, with the added influence of weight restrictions, may have overhead strained wires or a light plastic pergola.

Style is about individual choice. Have what you wish, but remember that the most successful constructions are always based on sound design principles rather than short-lived trends.

CONVENTIONAL MATERIALS

Timber – the most common medium for arches and pergolas – is available in many forms. Treated softwood is used widely for both posts and beams and is usually supplied as rough-sawn timber. Planed timber is smoother, ready to be painted with a choice of coloured wood stains.

▲ COTTAGE GARDEN ARCHWAY
The angled panels on either side of this square wooden arch make the structure resemble a bridge, reinforcing a sense of transition.

▼ IRON ROSE ARCH
Although iron is often an effective material for modern arches, here it has been worked to make a traditional Victorian-style rose arch.

RUSTIC ARCHES

- Such arches have a nostalgic old-world charm, most appropriate in cottage gardens.
- One significant drawback, however, is that they are seldom very robust and long-lasting.
- Leaving the bark on round poles achieves a particularly rustic look, but be aware that this will shorten their life still further.
- Prolong the life of a rustic arch by stripping the bark off the base of the posts and dipping them in preservative before setting them into the ground.
- Rustic arches will not support the weight of heavy climbers such as the rambling roses.

Hardwoods, particularly oak, are more durable and weather attractively to look especially good with older houses. Such woods tend to be more expensive. If they are your choice, ensure your purchase has been sourced from sustainable, managed forests.

Timber, for overhead beams or rafters, is often combined with other materials, which form the supporting piers. Bricks are a popular choice; they can have the advantage of matching the house walls. Small, cut blocks of natural stone, known as dressed stone, may also be used and although (as with bricks) construction can be slow and expensive, the result is usually worth it. Reconstituted stone is similar, but cheaper.

> ### Paint planed timber with a coloured stain for a modern architectural look

Wrought iron has traditionally been used to form rose arches, arbours, and pergola tunnels, and is still perfect in the right setting. Plastic-coated, tubular steel is the modern equivalent, which can be just as effective, if more flimsy. These light arches have the added benefit of remaining cool in hot climates, which protects the planting.

▲ EDIBLE ATTRACTION
A simple tubular steel arch, plastic coated to prevent the steel from overheating and so protecting the plants, is all that is needed to show off these gourds to dramatic effect.

▶ STEEL ARCHWAY
The entrance to this vegetable garden is framed by a tall, stately steel archway, containing the view and leading you from one part of the garden to the other.

ALTERNATIVE CHOICES

Reclaimed timber is a useful alternative to freshly sawn wood. Salvage yards stock all sorts of materials, including old beams, already attactively weathered. Machine-rounded poles associate well with decking and waterside gardens, while painted steel poles make a bold statement (*see p.12*), particularly when not softened by plants.

Box-section steel posts and steel girders are most effective used as part of pared-down minimalist designs, and even concrete lintels can be set into walls, forming sturdy overhead beams to support heavy climbers.

▶ RUSTIC ARCH
This rustic wooden arch over a meandering woodland path has an evocative charm, but such a structure may not last very long.

▼ MIXED MATERIALS
The flowers of Clematis 'Perle d'Azur' all but obscure the wrought iron arch supported by brick piers: a truly successful combination.

PLANTS FOR ARCHES AND PERGOLAS

COVERING ARCHES AND PERGOLAS with plants will provide vertical interest outside and will often form a good visual link between the house and garden. Climbers fulfil many functions in the garden, especially when associated with arches and pergolas; not only can they give exotic fragrances and colour, but they can also help provide dappled shade and privacy for seating areas.

DIFFERENT HABITS OF CLIMBERS

Climbing plants grow in several different ways. There are those, such as ivy, that climb by means of aerial roots, and those – like Virginia creeper (*Parthenocissus*) – that stick to the wall with suckers. By their very nature these plants tend to stay flat to a wall and, while they may be ideal on solid brick arches, they are less suitable for covering structures made of wood or metal. For these, twining plants are preferable as they will not only cover all sides of the posts, but will also reach from beam to beam, giving a greater coverage of foliage and consequently more shade.

Some plants, such as passion flowers, twine around posts by sending out tendrils,

ANNUAL CLIMBERS

• Provide interest while slower-growing permanent plants establish.
• Some fast-growing tender climbers can be grown as annuals in areas of winter cold; they can be enjoyed without needing to over-winter.
• Can be trained through permanent climbers or shrubs to keep interest through the seasons.
• Offer shade in summer but disappear to let in more light during winter.

while the whole stem of other plants, such as honeysuckle, winds around posts and beams. However they cling, all climbers benefit from a helping hand when planted; tie them onto vertical wires attached to the pergola posts (*see p.68*). For most plants,

NATURAL ARCHWAY
Clematis climbs using tendrils which twine around posts or, as in this case, other plants. Here the stems of Philadelphus (*mock orange*) *provide support for this clematis and together they form a natural archway into the garden beyond.*

this is sufficient assistance and they will soon start climbing, but roses in particular may need to be tied in more often: they will climb readily only if there are other host plants into which they can hook their thorns.

Many woody climbers, especially wisteria and many of the climbing roses,

> Large, heavy climbers like wisteria need the support of a sturdy pergola

are extremely heavy when mature, and need the support of a very sturdy framework. Do consider what plants you would like to grow when choosing an arch or pergola; some simple kits may not be robust enough for your ideal plant choice.

RAPID COVERAGE
Fast or short-term cover may be provided by annual climbers, many of which have the added benefit of flower and fragrance; sweet peas (*Lathyrus*) are a good example.

▲ HEAVYWEIGHT WISTERIA
A stout framework, such as that of this solidly built pergola, is needed to support the weight of the elegant, but vigorous, wisteria.

▼ AVENUE OF LABURNUM ARCHES
This inspirational golden archway is formed by training laburnum trees over steel arches, its style reminiscent of traditional tree arbours.

▲ MORNING GLORY
The twining annual Ipomoea
tricolor *'Heavenly Blue' has a
superb flower display from
summer to early autumn.*

▶ GOLDEN HOP
*A simple arbour is brightened
and covered quickly by the
fast-growing golden hop
(*Humulus lupulus *'Aureus').*

Certain herbaceous climbers are useful for
growing over simple structures near houses
or in roof gardens, where the summer
foliage will provide shade and shelter but,
in winter when the growth has died back,
the bare structure allows more light into
adjacent rooms. Hop (*Humulus*) is a fine
example of such a climber.

> ### Evergreen climbers offer both cover and privacy throughout the year

If fast coverage for screening is your
priority, choose carefully, as vigour can be
a short-lived virtue. The infamous mile-a-
minute (*Fallopia baldschuanica*) will
undoubtedly cover a pergola extremely
quickly, but it will soon engulf anything
else growing nearby as well. *Clematis*

montana or many of the honeysuckles,
while fast growing, will be less invasive and
much more attractive as well.

Evergreen climbers, such as *Clematis
armandii*, are useful for giving both cover
and privacy throughout the year.

Growing a number of climbers at once
can guarantee year-round interest, but it is
not always necessary to swamp an arch
with climbers: sometimes a single specimen
looks more effective. This is especially true
of a plant like the white wisteria, *Wisteria
floribunda* 'Alba', whose long clusters of
fragrant pea-flowers hang down from
overhead beams in an impressive display.

TAKING CARE OF YOUR PLANTING
It is important to note a plant's preferred
site and conditions before you make your
selection, to ensure your proposed position
fulfils its basic requirements. Once planted,
all climbing plants require some routine

▲ LILAC SOLANUM
Evergreen in mild areas, the fast-growing Solanum crispum *'Glasnevin' provides a lovely summer display of flowers.*

◄ TRUMPET VINE
From late summer to autumn, the sun-loving deciduous climber Campsis × tagliabuana *produces interesting orange-pink trumpet-shaped flowers.*

maintenance to keep them healthy and control their growth (*see p.68*).

Climbers produce a lot of growth from a small root ball, so will need regular watering and feeding. A thick layer of organic mulch such as composted bark, garden compost, or rotted manure, will help retain moisture and keep the roots cool, something that is especially important for all clematis, whose roots must be kept shaded, even when the top growth prefers sun. Evergreen climbers tend to be tidier than deciduous plants, and have the advantage of few fallen leaves to deal with.

Some climbers need tying in and many need pruning, particularly early on, to keep them in check unless of course, the desired effect is one of wild abandon.

CLIMBERS FOR SPEEDY COVERAGE

CLIMBERS TO GROW AS ANNUALS

Eccremocarpus scaber (Chilean glory flower) Ferny leaves, spikes of tubular orange flowers.
Lathyrus odoratus (Sweet pea) Strongly scented flowers in many colours.
Rhodochiton (Purple bell vine) Tubular purple flowers with mauve-pink calyx all summer.
Thunbergia (Black-eyed Susan) Heart-shaped leaves and black-centred orange flowers through summer into autumn.

FAST-GROWING CLIMBERS

Clematis montana var. *rubens* Masses of pink flowers in late spring.
Parthenocissus tricuspidata (Boston ivy) Ivy-like leaves, brilliant crimson in autumn. Has suckers so only suitable for brick or stone.
Passiflora caerulea (Passion flower) Intricate flowers from summer into autumn, then orange seed pods.
Solanum crispum 'Glasnevin' Purple star-shaped summer flowers. Evergreen in mild areas.

PLANTS FOR SUNSHINE AND SHADE

IT IS EASY TO ASSUME that, because many pergolas stand over warm terraces or are built to create shaded walkways, many of the plants shrouding them will survive only in open sunny positions. In fact, arches and pergolas are not always to be found in warm, light sites, and arbours are often deliberately set in cool, wooded areas. Fortunately, there are climbing plants to suit both extremes.

PLANTS FOR SUN

Most climbers benefit from the light and heat that is reflected from walls and terraces. The sun-loving climbers growing over pergolas in these open, warm positions tend to be eye-catching plants with strong flower interest. Among the showiest are the many roses, clematis, grape vines, and wisterias.

To ensure their dramatic summer show, many of these climbers must be hard-pruned in early spring, leaving the supports bare. For permanent cover you may wish to grow them with an evergreen climber.

Several grape vines have good foliage and are suited to growing over a pergola; many need no competition from other plants. In cooler areas, the grapes may not develop fully outdoors.

Wisteria, with its scented hanging flowers, is unsurpassed for style and elegance. In mild climates, few sights are as showy as the vibrant colours of a bougainvillea, especially draped over a pergola.

▲ *CLEMATIS* 'JACKMANII'
The large, wonderful, velvety purple flowers of this sun-loving clematis appear from mid- to late summer.

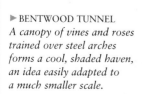

► BENTWOOD TUNNEL
A canopy of vines and roses trained over steel arches forms a cool, shaded haven, an idea easily adapted to a much smaller scale.

▲ YELLOW VARIEGATED IVY
*Like all ivies, 'Goldheart' is
shade tolerant. It adds a splash
of colour to the dullest corners.*

◄ CLIMBING HYDRANGEA
*Although slow to establish,
this shade-tolerant climber
becomes vigorous. Its lacecap
flowers appear in summer.*

PLANTS FOR SHADE

Arbours and pergolas sited in shady parts
of the garden require climbers tolerant of
lower light levels. Many shade-tolerant
climbers grow naturally in woodland in the
wild. Shade-tolerant self-clinging climbers
are ideal for growing on solid brick or
stone archways in these conditions. One of
the best plants of this type is the deciduous,
climbing hydrangea, (*Hydrangea anomala*
subsp. *petiolaris*).

Many of the ivies are also suitable for
scrambling over arches and arbours in
shady positions. The white- and yellow-
variegated forms are particularly useful to
brighten up dark corners.

Honeysuckles are twining plants that
originate in woodland conditions, and so
make ideal climbers for shaded pergolas
and arbours. Many are evergreen,
providing all-year cover, with most being
fast-growing and fragrant as well. Not all
clematis need to be grown in full sun either.
C. montana is a vigorous, late-spring-
flowering climber tolerant of shade; it has
pink- and white-flowered forms.

CLIMBERS TO SUIT YOUR SITE

PLANTS FOR FULL SUN

Campis radicans Red or yellow trumpet
flowers from late summer to early autumn.
Rosa 'Madame Grégoire Staechelin' Pink,
slightly fragrant flower clusters in summer.
Vitis vinifera 'Purpurea' Strong growing vine
with deep red leaves, richer in autumn.
Wisteria sinensis Lilac flowers; needs plenty
of space. White-flowered **W. floribunda 'Alba'**
is less vigorous.

PLANTS FOR SHADE

Clematis armandii Fragrant white flowers in
early spring; evergreen in a sheltered position.
Hedera colchica 'Dentata Variegata' and **H.
helix 'Goldheart'** Variegated ivies. Evergreen.
Lonicera japonica 'Halliana' Fast-growing
fragrant, evergreen honeysuckle.
Schizophragma integrifolium White summer
flowers, heart-shaped leaves. Climbs by aerial
roots so best on brick or stone.

FRAGRANT CLIMBERS

W HEN CHOOSING CLIMBERS to clothe arches and pergolas, fragrance is, for many people, the overriding criterion. Enduring images of rose-covered arbours, pergolas dripping with headily scented wisteria, or arches clothed in sweet-smelling honeysuckle are very appealing. There are others aside from these three classics, and not all of them require sunny conditions to do well.

SOME SCENTED FAVOURITES

Jasmine – especially *Jasmine officinale* f. *affine*, with pink flowers flushed white – is among the best pergola climbers, for both fragrance and visual appeal. A twisting semi-evergreen, it gives a dense cover in sun and produces a strong, heady scent through summer. *Clematis flammula* is a vigorous, herbaceous clematis that needs cutting down every winter; however bare it is in the early months, the almond-scented white flowers, in late summer and early autumn, more than compensate. The chocolate vine, (*Akebia quinata*), is an interesting, semi-evergreen, twining climber, best in sun. Vanilla-scented reddish purple flowers appear in late spring and ripen to purple, sausage-shaped fruits.

▲ WHITE WISTERIA
The lovely white Wisteria floribunda *'Alba' flowers in early summer. Give it plenty of space, since the plant is extremely vigorous.*

► HONEYSUCKLE ARCH
The fragrance of honeysuckle, particularly heady at dusk, encourages anyone passing through to pause a while to survey the view beyond.

FRAGRANT CLIMBING ROSES

Roses in all forms are often chosen for their perfume. Happily, a huge selection of fragrant climbing roses, suitable for training over pergolas and arches, exists. Particularly fine examples are *Rosa* 'Wedding Day' (extremely vigorous rambling rose with masses of repeat-flowering, creamy white blooms), *R.* 'New Dawn' (less vigorous, with strongly scented pale pink flowers) and *R.* 'Madame Alfred Carrière' (even paler pink, and suitable for structures on the shady sides of gardens).

MORE FRAGRANT CLIMBERS

Actinidia kolomikta Twisting, with variegated leaves and small white summer flowers.

Clematis armandii (almond-scented) and *C. montana* 'Elizabeth' (vanilla-scented).

Lonicera Many, in particular *L.* x *americana*, *L.* x *brownii* 'Dropmore Scarlet', *L. japonica* 'Halliana', and *L. periclymenum* 'Serotina'.

Rosa Many, including *R.* 'Albertine', *R.* 'Compassion', *R.* 'Gloire de Dijon', and *R.* 'Zéphirine Drouhin' (thornless).

Trachelospermum jasminoides Creamy white fragrant flowers in summer.

Wisteria Many including *W.* x *formosa* and *W. sinensis*.

▲ *ROSA* 'NEW DAWN'
This attractive climbing rose has extremely fragrant, pale pink flowers from summer to autumn. It can be grown in shady gardens.

▼ JASMINE
The unmistakable scent of their star-flowers makes jasmine a popular choice, particularly for growing on pergolas over seating areas.

SEASONAL INTEREST

K EEPING INTEREST IN A GARDEN all year round can be a difficult job, especially in small gardens, where the view is of the whole. Larger gardens may have the luxury of different "rooms" for different times of the year. For both, the range of climbing plants available can, through flower, foliage, and fruits, ensure that appeal is maintained through all the seasons. Failing that, a well-designed arch or pergola can be a feature itself during the winter months.

SPRING CLIMBERS
Many clematis are among the earliest flowering climbers to enliven pergolas and archways; *Clematis alpina* 'Frances Rivis' has pale blue flowers followed by fluffy seedheads. It tolerates exposed conditions and lower light levels than other varieties. A more vigorous clematis for this time of year is *C. montana* 'Elizabeth', whose soft pink, scented flowers appear in late spring.

SUMMER INTEREST
This is the time of year that offers the most choice, and is the season when most people want to be outside enjoying their gardens.

Fragrant climbers come into their own in summer, especially when planted around seating areas. A good example is the star jasmine (*Trachelospermum jasminoides*),

▲ HOT PINK AND TURQUOISE BOWER
Although bougainvillea is too tender to survive outdoors all year except in the mildest areas, it never fails to make a dramatic statement.

◄ SPRING PROFUSION OF CLEMATIS
Clematis montana f. grandiflora *is a very vigorous, hardy climber that produces an abundance of white flowers in spring.*

▲ CLEMATIS SEEDHEADS IN WINTER
Fluffy seedheads follow the yellow autumn flowers of Clematis tangutica, *and provide a welcome extra dimension late in the season.*

◄ *VITIS COIGNETIAE*
This vigorous vine is at its most striking in autumn, when the large heart-shaped leaves turn brilliant red. Like all vines, it is hardy.

which has small, fragrant white flowers, followed by seed pods. It is an evergreen climber and, in a sheltered site, provides good screening. *Actinidia kolomikta* is a deciduous, twining climber. Its green leaves are tipped with pink and white, as though they have been dipped into pots of paint.

Many of the honeysuckles (*Lonicera*) are useful summer climbers as they are vigorous, rapidly covering any overhead structure. Most are scented and evergreen, too. *L. japonica* var. *repens*, for example, has all these attributes, and an interesting,

purple flush in the leaves and flowers. Roses, in many forms, can always be relied upon for summer flowers and fragrance.

AUTUMN AND WINTER

Several climbers, notably vines (*Vitis*) and Virginia creeper (*Parthenocissus*) colour dramatically in autumn, clothing arches and pergolas with their vibrant oranges and reds.

Few climbing plants, apart from ivy and other evergreens, have much of interest in winter. An exception is the winter-flowering evergreen, *Clematis cirrhosa* var. *balearica*.

MORE CLIMBERS FOR SEASONAL INTEREST

SPRING	SUMMER	AUTUMN/WINTER
Akebia quinata Vanilla-scented purple-brown flowers in late spring; followed by purple fruit. *Clematis armandii* Evergreen climber with small fragrant white flowers. *Schisandra rubriflora* Deciduous twining plant, small red flowers.	*Berberidopsis corallina* Red flowers. Evergreen. *Clematis* 'Nelly Moser' Large pink-and-white striped flowers. *Lonicera* Many, especially *L. japonica* 'Aureoreticulata' and *L. periclymenum* 'Graham Thomas'. *Rosa* Many. *Wisteria* Many.	*Campsis* x *tagliabuana* 'Madame Galen' Orange-red trumpet-shaped flowers. *Clematis tangutica* Fluffy seedheads follow yellow lantern shaped flowers. *Vitis vinifera* 'Purpurea', *V. coignetiae*

ERECTING ARCHES AND PERGOLAS

BUILDING FROM KITS

IF DO-IT-YOURSELF is not your strong point, or time and money are limited, have a look at kit-form arches and pergolas. They are less expensive than custom-made structures, and quick and simple enough for relatively inexperienced people to put together. The convenience of picking up a pergola in a store is appealing, especially since good design need not be sacrificed for the sake of convenience.

CHOOSING A STYLE

Before buying a kit, consider the style of your house and garden, and the proposed site for your arch or pergola. Measure exactly how much space you have to ensure that the structure is not too small or big for its surroundings. Consider how easy the kit is to construct, and your own level of experience. In general, some of the bolt-together timber kits look better with newer housing while black tubular steel constructions may be more suited to a traditional setting. All structures may look stark until softened by climbers.

MAKE YOUR MARK *Numerous styles of kit pergolas are available, and can be customized further by painting them in a colour of your choice. Here, the cool grey blends well with the restful greens of the surrounding woodland planting.*

◀ METAL ARCH *This arch is unobtrusive, but strong enough to support the advancing roses.*

BUYING KITS

Arches, pergolas, and arbours in kit form are available from garden centres, superstores, and by mail order. Most suppliers produce detailed catalogues, providing a picture of the finished structure and exact dimensions, and showing components that allow you to customize your design by combining different elements. Kits may be in treated timber or plastic-coated tubular steel. It is a good idea to go shopping with a clear idea of what you want.

WHAT DO YOU NEED?

Although building from kits is much simpler than starting from scratch with raw timber, practical skills and experience are still useful when kit-form pergolas and arches are assembled. Detailed instructions are always supplied as part of the kit; read these through before you start to ensure that you know what is expected of you and that it is within your capabilities. In-store help is usually available if you have any queries about construction or need further guidance as to what tools and other materials, such as metal post supports or optional trellis, are necessary to complete the job. You will certainly need a good set of measuring, digging, and woodworking tools (*see p.62*); make sure you have these before you start.

TIPS ON ASSEMBLY

• Do not plan to build the structure on the same day that it is delivered; it may arrive late, or have pieces missing.
• Lay all the components out and check them off against the materials list.
• Be clear as to what all the different items are as some parts can look similar to each other.
• Make sure you have all the necessary tools before starting. If a list is not supplied, compile your own from the instructions.
• The job will be much easier with two people.
• Follow the written instructions, step-by-step.
• Do not fully tighten any nuts and bolts until you are satisfied that the structure is complete.

EXAMPLES OF KITS
Timber kits for arches and pergolas are usually bundled into easily identified packs of component parts such as those shown here. Some components, like the arbour seat in the pack second from the left, come pre-assembled, ready to be slotted into place.

PREPARATION AND ASSEMBLY

Before you start, make sure that your site is clear and level. Putting together a kit, especially for the first time, can be a fiddly job, so allow yourself plenty of time – in fact, probably twice as long as you think you will need. Begin by double-checking all the details, particularly measurements, as this can save you a lot of effort in the long run; refer to the supplier's tools and materials list to ensure that you have all the right component parts and correct equipment for their assembly. Ideally, two people are better than one when the time comes to carry out the work. At the very least, enlist some help for jobs above head height, and for those jobs where heavy or awkward pieces need to be lifted or carried. Remember that simple, lightweight components such as those used in Simple Wooden Arch (*see pp.41–44*) can often be put together more easily on the ground. Most kits must be constructed in a certain order, so do not guess but follow the instructions step-by-step and extremely carefully.

▲ METAL POST SUPPORTS AND DRIVING TOOL
These spiked post supports are driven into the ground to hold timber posts firm and prevent them from rotting at ground level.

▼ CHECK ALL PARTS
Lay out all the component parts when the kit arrives, and check each item against the supplier's materials list.

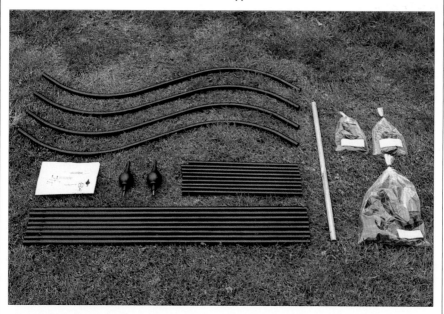

METAL ARCH

There are great advantages in choosing an arch made from plastic-coated tubular steel, and there are many styles available in kit form. In spite of their lightweight framework, such arches are extremely strong, will not have to be painted to prevent rust, and can be delivered to your home. The component parts interlock, providing a whole array of styles that will enable you to create an arch designed to your own specification. If you would like something more substantial, you can commission a blacksmith to make a traditional metal arch, or a more modern structure of steel posts or girders. The instructions here are for a classic Gothic-style arch, 1.2m (4ft) wide and 2.4m (8ft) tall.

ADVANTAGES OF METAL
- Lightweight tubular steel structures can be erected by just one person.
- The slender posts can highlight the plants rather than the structure itself.
- Steel posts, although thin, are very strong.

YOU NEED:

TOOLS
Screwdriver • Allen key, as supplied • Holemaker, as supplied • Hammer • Spirit level

MATERIALS
- 8 uprights, as supplied
- 8 moisture seals, as supplied
- 18 T-joints, as supplied
- 4 hoops, as supplied
- 9 spacer bars, 1 shorter, as supplied
- 2 parallel clamps, as supplied
- 2 finials, as supplied
- Nuts, bolts, and washers

PARTS OF A METAL ARCH

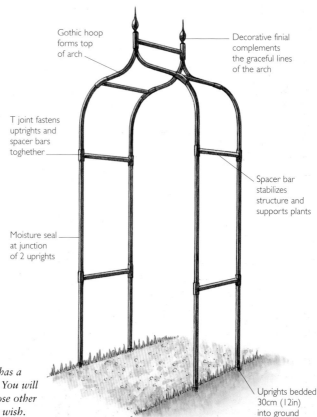

Gothic hoop forms top of arch

Decorative finial complements the graceful lines of the arch

T joint fastens uptrights and spacer bars toghether

Spacer bar stabilizes structure and supports plants

Moisture seal at junction of 2 uprights

Uprights bedded 30cm (12in) into ground

TUBULAR METAL ARCH
This tubular metal arch has a Gothic detail at the top. You will probably be able to choose other shapes for the top if you wish.

◀PLANT-FREE FEATURE *Stark but stylish, this white-painted arch highlights the garden entrance.*

ASSEMBLING THE FRAME

1 **Once you have unpacked** the kit and checked each item against the instructions to see that all parts are there, separate the 8 upright sections, and 4 of the moisture seals. Place a seal over 1 end of 4 of the uprights.

2 **Insert 1 end of** the remaining 4 uprights firmly into each of the moisture seals from step 1. This will form the 4 straight sections of the arch: the front and back of both the left and right sides.

3 **Slide 2 T-joints down** each of the 4 upright sections. Loosely screw the T-joints into position an even distance apart. Join a front upright section to a back section with 2 of the spacer bars by inserting them into the T-joints.

4 **Repeat with the other** front and back upright sections. The spacer bars hold the arch together and prevent it from twisting. You may find it easier to fit the spacer bars by balancing the uprights on the ground.

5 **Assemble the top** section in a similar way. Fit 2 spacer bars to each hooped front and back, and join the 2 sides together at the top with the short spacer bar and a parallel clamp at each end. Secure the clamps with nuts and bolts and tighten with the Allen key. Fix the finials between the parallel clamps.

ERECTING THE ARCH

2 Knock the metal holemaker into each of the 4 post positions to the marked depth with a club hammer. Then, remove the holemaker carefully. The hole-maker should be marked at the correct depth, but if it is not, make your own marking to ensure each hole is exactly the same depth, about 30cm (12in) deep.

1 Place the top of the arch on the ground precisely where you want the arch to stand, to locate the positions for the uprights. Be careful to keep dirt out of the open tube ends.

3 Set the 2 sides of the arch into the holes. Use a spirit level to check that the posts are vertically set. Slide a moisture seal onto the top of each post, then set the top hooped section into these seals to complete the arch.

FINISHED GOTHIC ARCH
Once the arch is constructed, check that the spacer bars are level and exactly opposite, then tighten all the nuts and bolts.

SIMPLE WOODEN ARCH

A wooden arch is simple to construct, and when built from treated timber it makes a long-lasting support for plants. Whether the roof is pitched, as below, flat and pergola-like, or rounded, the procedure remains the same; mark out the area, assemble and erect posts and beams, then place the rafters on the top. These instructions are for a kit with 2.4m (8ft) posts set 1.2m (4ft) apart left to right, and 30cm (1ft) deep.

WORKING WITH TIMBER

• Use treated timber, and paint sawn ends with preservative to prolong the life of the wood.
• Use metal "shoes": they prevent the bottom of timber posts from rotting in damp ground.
• Always fix joists with galvanized nails or rustproof screws.
• Never saw timber joists in the air on a step ladder; always remove to ground level, and saw on a firm bench.
• Use a wooden mallet or hammer and wooden block to avoid damaging the timber.

YOU NEED:

TOOLS
• Set square
• Hammer or mallet
• Club hammer
• Marking pegs
• String
• Driving tool
• Spirit level
• Drill
• Screwdriver

MATERIALS
• 4 spiked metal post supports or "shoes"
• 4 lengths of treated, sawn timber for beams, as supplied
• 4 lengths of treated, sawn timber for posts, as supplied
• 6 lengths of treated, sawn timber for rafters, as supplied
• Rustproof screws or galvanized nails
• Wood preservative

PARTS OF AN ARCH

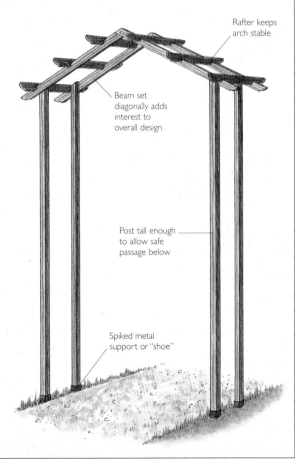

Rafter keeps arch stable

Beam set diagonally adds interest to overall design

Post tall enough to allow safe passage below

Spiked metal support or "shoe"

▶ POST AND BEAM ARCH
This simple wooden arch has square sawn posts fixed in metal supports, a pitched roof, and evenly spaced rafters.

◀ ARCH OVER A PATH *This sturdy timber arch is simple to construct and will last a long time.*

MARKING OUT THE AREA

1 Use a large set square or framing square to measure out the exact position of the archway: this ensures that the 2 sides of the arch are parallel to each other and that the front and back are square to the sides. Using a mallet, drive in a marking peg at 2 corners, winding the string around the outside of the peg.

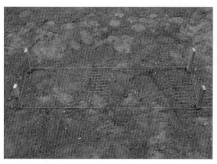

2 Measure and mark the opposite corners. Draw the string line taut along the sides of the framing square. Check that you have measured accurately (always measure from the same points), adjusting the pegs if necessary.

3 Using a mallet and driving tool, hammer a spiked metal support for the arch posts into each of the 4 corners exactly where the measuring peg was. Check each one with a spirit level to ensure it stands upright.

CONSTRUCTING THE FRAME

1 First join the pitched beams. These lengths of timber for the back and front arch top should be cut in a half-lap joint (see p.65) at the correct angle for the arch: how steep this angle is determines the pitch of the roof.

2 Lay the 2 sections of timber for one side of the roof neatly together and, if the kit is not pre-drilled, drill 2 holes in the join. Fix with rustproof screws. Similarly, join the beams for the other side of the roof.

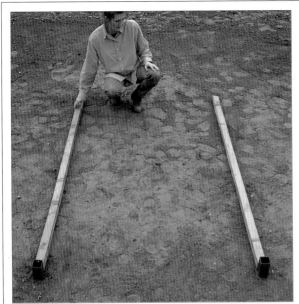

3 Lay out the posts for one side on the ground, and butt them up firmly to the metal supports to hold them steady, and to confirm they will be exactly parallel once erected. This also allows you to fix the top of the arch to the posts while they are still on firm ground, rather than balancing high up on a step ladder. This is only possible where the posts are not too heavy to lift once assembled.

4 Make sure the beam end overlaps the 2 post tops by the same amount. Drill 2 holes in the first post, and secure to the beam with rustproof screws. Drill and fix the second post and beam.

5 Repeat for the posts and beams on the opposite side; take care to attach each set of beams to the outer side of the posts. The two sides of the arch are now ready to set up.

SETTING UP THE FRAME AND PLACING RAFTERS

1 **With a helper,** lift up the front of the arch and lower the posts into their supports. Repeat for the back. Check that the posts are straight, then screw each one into its support.

2 **Measure out** and mark where the notched rafters should lie when evenly spaced apart. Hammer each end into place using a block of wood to protect the rafter.

3 **Tap the rafters** down until they fit tightly onto the beams. Fix the rafters at both ends to the beams using galvanized nails.

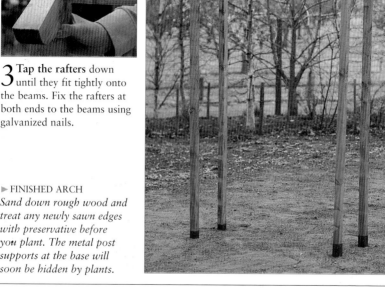

▶ FINISHED ARCH
Sand down rough wood and treat any newly sawn edges with preservative before you plant. The metal post supports at the base will soon be hidden by plants.

CREATING A ROSE TRELLIS ARCH

Traditional rose-covered archways look wonderful, especially in a country setting, framing entrances into flower or vegetable gardens. One of the easiest ways to make such an archway is to extend a simple wooden arch by adding trellis panels. These panels create a framework onto which rambling roses (or other climbing plants) will grow, and by enclosing the arch on either side in this way, the mystery of the space beyond will be maintained. The following instructions are based on a simple wooden arch kit with 2.4m (8ft) posts (*see pp.41–4*).

TIPS WITH TRELLIS

• Buy pre-assembled trellis panels to save time; trim to the required size if necessary.

• Use treated trellis panels in the arch and for the side panels; newly sawn edges should be smoothed down and treated with preservative.

• Choose between squares and diamonds for a different effect, painted if you wish.

• Support trellis panels in a level position with blocks of wood before fixing.

• Use finials on post tops to provide a smart finishing touch.

ROSE TRELLIS ARCH
Trellis panels enhance and transform a plain arch into a real feature. The diamond pattern is carried through and echoed in the gate.

YOU NEED:

TOOLS
• As for Simple Wooden Arch (*see p.41*)

MATERIALS
• As for Simple Wooden Arch (*see p.41*)
• 2 narrow sections of treated timber trellis panels, suggest 1.8m (6ft) tall
• 2 large square trellis panels, suggest 1.2m (4ft) tall
• 2 spiked metal post supports or "shoes"
• 2 treated timber posts, at least 7.5x7.5cm (3x3in), suggest 1.35m (4½ft) tall
• 8 galvanized panel clips
• Rustproof screws and nails
• 2 ball finials (*optional*)
• Sandpaper
• Wood preservative

STARTING WITH YOUR ARCH

STARTING POINT
The basic wooden arch may be extended into a traditional rose arch; slot narrow sections of trellis between the front and back posts and add a trellis panel to each side of the existing arch.

ATTACHING THE TRELLIS PANELS

1 **Trim the narrow** sections of trellis to size if necessary, and slot into the side of the arch, keeping the base just above ground level. Check the panel is straight, and screw to the top, middle, and bottom of both posts (*inset*).

2 **To determine the** exact position of the supporting post, hold the side trellis panel absolutely flush between the front arch post and the shoe of the metal support. Mark precisely where the post support should be.

3 **Set the panel aside.** Drive the metal post support into the ground with the driving tool, or a block of wood. Insert the post, check that it is straight, and screw into the support.

4 **Slot the panel in,** keeping it above ground and level with blocks of wood. Mark where the panel clips will go (in line with trellis cross beams) near the top and base of the new post.

5 **Nail the** panel clips to the the post, top and bottom where marked. Repeat exactly opposite on front arch post.

6 **Slot the panel** into the clips from above. Screw the 4 clips to the cross beams of the trellis panel.

7 **If you wish,** screw in a ball, acorn, or other style finial on each post to provide a neat finishing touch.

◀ FINISHED TRELLIS ARCH
When you have done one side of the arch, erect the trellis panels on the other side in exactly the same way. After all four panels are completed, it is wise to check that the posts are firm and that the panel clips are screwed tight. Sand down any rough edges and treat any cut and exposed ends of timber with preservative. You are now ready to plant the climbing or rambling roses of your choice.

FREESTANDING WOODEN PERGOLA

A freestanding timber structure is probably the most common type of pergola. It is a simple construction of posts supporting beams and rafters. As with arches, many pergola kits are available today for the do-it-yourself market. Assembly of these is much simplified; timbers are pre-notched, edges are planed, and corner braces may even be glued into place for you. These instructions are for a kit with 2.4m (8ft) posts set 1.2m (4ft) apart left to right, and 55cm (22in) deep.

WOODEN PERGOLAS

• To guarantee long life, always use sawn timber that has been pre-treated to last, and avoid rustic pole constructions.
• Treated sawn timber will always look better than rough cut wood.
• Space rafters close together to cast more shade. For a light and airy structure, make the spacings between the rafters wider.
• For a traditional effect, choose beams with shaped ends. For a contemporary look, choose beams with square ends.
• Always make pergolas sturdy; even though they may appear stark and heavy, this will be hidden once covered in established climbers.

YOU NEED:

TOOLS
• As for Simple Wooden Arch (see p.41)

MATERIALS
• 4 spiked post supports
• 4 treated, sawn timber posts, as supplied
• 2 lengths of treated, sawn timber for beams, as supplied
• 4 lengths of treated, sawn timber for rafters, as supplied
• 4 lengths of treated, sawn timber for braces, as supplied
• Rustproof nails and galvanized screws

PARTS OF A PERGOLA

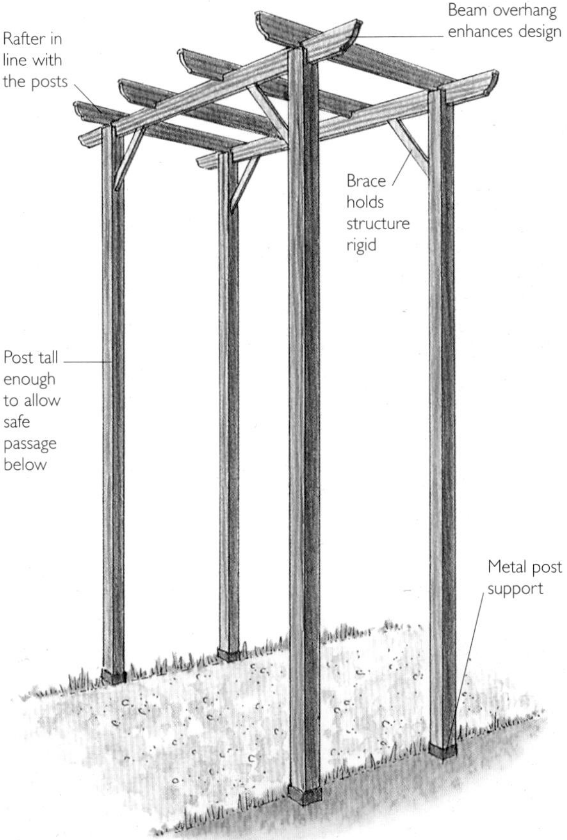

Rafter in line with the posts

Beam overhang enhances design

Brace holds structure rigid

Post tall enough to allow safe passage below

Metal post support

▶ POST-AND-BEAM PERGOLA
This drawing shows a standard pergola construction with square sawn posts in metal supports, supporting beams and evenly spaced rafters.

◀ ADDED ATTRACTION *A well-made pergola lends vertical interest to a woodland path.*

SECURING METAL POST SUPPORTS

1 **Measure the** position of the posts by following Marking Out the Area (*see p.42, steps 1–3*). Hammer in the metal post supports.

2 **Using a spirit** level, keep checking that the post supports remain vertical as you hammer them in. Ensure they face exactly square on.

ERECTING THE FRAME

2 **Knock both ends** of one the cross beams into the notches cut into the top of the 2 front posts, making sure the overhang is the same on both sides. Repeat with the back beam.

1 **Insert the posts** into the supports, making sure the notches at the top all run in the direction that the beams will lie. Check the posts are vertical, and screw to the supports.

3 **When you are** happy that the beams are positioned correctly, that is standing proud of the post tops, overhangs even on both sides, nail them to the posts.

4 **Once fixed** to each corner post, the 2 parallel cross beams are ready to receive the 4 overhead rafters. It is better not to assemble large, heavy posts on the ground first as was advised in the Simple Arch (*see p.45*).

5 **Position a rafter** above the left posts, then place another over the right posts. Measure and mark the position of the 2 central rafters so that they will be evenly spaced and parallel.

6 **Tap the** notched rafters down onto the beams at the marked even spacings. Secure each rafter to the front and back beams using nails or screws.

7 **To strengthen** and steady the pergola, nail a timber brace into each top corner between post and beam.

▶ FINISHED PERGOLA
Lightly sand rough edges and treat any cut ends of timber with preservative. The pergola is now ready for planting.

CREATING AN ARBOUR

A simple pergola construction can be turned into an arbour by adding trellis panels on three sides. You can place a bench or other seat in this enclosure or you can build an integral bench instead; many pergolas with integral benches are available in kit form. Climbing plants can be tied to the trellis for support, and fragrant types are particularly desirable. Additional trellis panels built onto the side of the arbour ensure that the structure links into the surrounding planting; cover these with climbers as well. Be aware that flimsy do-it-yourself arbours will not last as long as more solid constructions. Some companies sell and install magnificent hardwood structures, but they are expensive. The following instructions are based on an arbour with integral bench in kit form.

PERGOLA TO ARBOUR

- Site the arbour against a backdrop of shrubs, and to give views across the garden.
- Build a bench across the narrow part of the pergola; this could make a sitting place at the far end of a covered walkway.
- Additional side trellis panels for climbers will give a link with the adjacent planting.
- Use smooth planed timber for the integral seat to avoid splinters.

YOU NEED:

TOOLS
- As for Simple Arch (*see p.41*)

MATERIALS
- As for Free-standing Wooden Pergola (*see p.49*)
- 2 backrest supports, as supplied
- 2 seat supports, as supplied
- Planed timber seat and backrest, as supplied
- 2 spiked metal post supports
- 2 treated timber posts, as supplied
- 5 trellis panels, as supplied: 2 narrow for sides, 1 large for back, 2 medium for front

▶ FINISHED PERGOLA
The timber pergola shown on pp.49–51 is the starting point for the arbour.

START WITH A FREESTANDING PERGOLA

◀ARBOUR RETREAT *Trellis panels flank this arbour set against a backdrop of shrubs.*

FIXING IN THE SEAT

1 **Start by joining** 1 backrest support and 1 beam to support the seat together by means of a simple half-lap joint (*see p.65*). The angle at which this joint is cut determines the slope of the backrest.

2 **Fix the 2 pieces of wood,** which should be planed and sanded for a neat, tight joint, together with a galvanized nail. Repeat this sequence for the beam and backrest support for the other side.

3 **Decide what** height you want your bench to be – ideally about 45cm (18in) above ground level. Remember that ground level may be higher if you pave beneath the seat at a later date. Screw the 2 seat supports to the inside of the pergola at the correct height first. Make sure the 2 supports are level with each other, and that the backrest support is flush on the back posts. Screw in (*inset*).

4 **Evenly spaced slats,** as supplied in the kit, are already fixed by screws to battens on either side for both the seat and backrest. Screw the backrest to the backrest support, making sure it is even along the top.

5 **Secure both sides** of the seat to the supporting beams in the same way as for the backrest in step 4.

◄ FINISHED ARBOUR
Trellis panels can then be fitted into the two sides and onto the back of the pergola to enclose the seat, and at right angles each side. Follow the steps for Attaching the Trellis Panels (see pp.46–47, steps 1–7). You can attach ball finials to the top of the posts (see p.47, step 7) if you wish.

WALL-LEANING PERGOLA

This style of pergola, sometimes known as a lean-to, is ideal for when you wish to create an area of shade or shelter directly adjacent to a house or other wall. It is fairly easy to construct, with fewer posts to erect than with a freestanding pergola. The overhead beams can either be attached to a timber wall plate – a length of timber bolted to the wall – or inserted into special metal fittings, called joist hangers, screwed into the brickwork.

YOU NEED:

TOOLS
- As for Simple Arch (see p.41).
- Power drill

MATERIALS
- 5 metal joist hangers
- Wall plugs
- 5 timber rafters, 2 timber posts, 1 timber beam; ensure all timber is treated
- Dome head galvanized screws with washers
- Locating screws

USING JOIST HANGERS TO FIX BEAMS

1 First, determine where the 2 free-standing posts will be. Mark the wall directly opposite, and at the correct height: this is where the first 2 joist hangers will go. Space the other 3 evenly at precisely the same height, and mark the position of their screw holes as well.

2 Use a power drill with a masonry bit to drill the screw holes in all the positions marked. Where possible, drill into a mortar joint, which is easier than drilling directly into brick.

3 When you have drilled all the holes, push a wall plug into each hole to give a firm fixing for the screw. Use a hammer to knock the wall plug in until it is flush with the brickwork.

4 Position each joist hanger and fix it to the wall using the dome head screws with washers. Ensure all screws fit tightly. Next, erect the 2 posts as for Freestanding Pergola (see p.50).

BEAMS OVERHEAD

- Joist hangers are best used on sound, flat brickwork.
- On worn surfaces, timber wall-plates provide a more secure and safer fixing.
- A cordless battery drill for drilling holes is safer and easier to use than an electric drill with a cable.
- When measuring the height of rafters, calculate any notches cut into the wood into your measurements.
- Widely spaced beams let in more light; narrow the spacings for more shade.

5 **Erect the beam** between the posts (*see p.50, steps 2–3*). Then, stretch each rafter from wall to beam, fitting one end into the joist hanger first.

6 **Once all the** rafters are in position – straight and level – insert a locating screw through the side of the joist hanger to hold the rafter firm.

USING TIMBER WALL-PLATES

Rafters may be attached to a wall-plate either by means of brackets screwed to the top of the wall-plate into which the beams are nailed (*right*); or by cutting notches in both pieces of wood (*far right*). Cut the notches in the wall-plate before bolting it to the wall.

WALL-PLATE WITH BRACKET

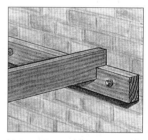

NOTCHED WALL-PLATE

◄ FINISHED WALL-LEANING PERGOLA
This simple lean-to pergola over a seating area on a small patio has two supporting posts and a cross beam, and five rafters fixed to a timber wall-plate against the rendered house wall.

BRICK POST PERGOLAS

Pergolas with brick posts (or piers) are ideal for larger gardens, where they can support fairly substantial beams, rafters, and heavy climbers. They have the added advantages of linking visually with brick-walled houses, and they offer a greater sense of permanence than less-substantial kit-constructions made of wood or metal. Constructing brick posts is a slow job but the effort will reward you with an attractive permanent feature. Proper footings (or foundations) are required, as are good bricklaying skills; this can make brick posts costly to commission. If you take on the work yourself, ensure that the brick courses are level and that the posts do not twist.

BUILDING BRICK POSTS
- Construct brick posts around a central, vertical reinforcing bar for strength.
- Ensure that the brick posts are built up to exactly the same height.
- Constantly check the brickwork is both square and vertical as the work progresses.
- Make piers no less than 32cm (13in) square.
- Low brick plinths protect the base of timber posts from rotting.

MAKING A BRICK-POST PERGOLA

Constructing a low brick pier around the base of each wooden post is simpler than building one at full height. The low coping (*see cross section, p.61*) makes a shelf for pots. Once you have completed your brick posts, follow the steps for Freestanding Wooden Pergola (*see pp.50–51*).

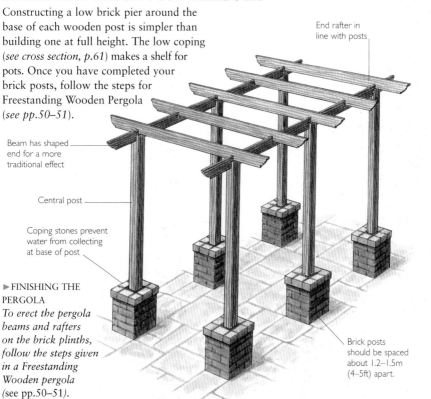

End rafter in line with posts

Beam has shaped end for a more traditional effect

Central post

Coping stones prevent water from collecting at base of post

▶FINISHING THE PERGOLA
To erect the pergola beams and rafters on the brick plinths, follow the steps given in a Freestanding Wooden pergola (see pp.50–51).

Brick posts should be spaced about 1.2–1.5m (4–5ft) apart.

◀NARROW BRICK PERGOLA *Even a short pergola adds depth as well as height to a small garden.*

YOU NEED:

TOOLS
• As for Simple Arch (*see p.41*)
• Spade or shovel
• Brick trowel
• Pointing trowel

MATERIALS
• Crushed stone for a hardcore base (*see p.64*)
• Concrete: 1 part cement to 6 parts aggregate mixed with water (*see p.64*)
• Treated, sawn timber posts
• Mortar: 1 part cement to 5 or 6 parts builder's sand mixed with water and plasticizer (*see p.64*)
• Weather-proof engineering, or well-fired stock, bricks

PREPARING THE FOUNDATION

1 **Decide where** the posts will be and dig a hole about 45cm (18in) square by 30cm (12in) deep for each one. Pour in a sub-base of hardcore (crushed stone), to fill half the depth when compacted.

2 **Set the post** into the centre of the hole and hold it vertical. Have a helper keep it upright, or use a temporary support if you are on your own, while you start to fill the hole with concrete.

LAYING THE BRICKS

1 **Fill with** concrete to ground level. Check the base of the post with a spirit level to ensure that it is exactly vertical. Leave the concrete to dry overnight.

2 **Now cover the** dry concrete with a layer of wet mortar. Start to bed the bricks onto the mortar around the base of the wooden post. Lay the bricks in a staggered bond, which will avoid vertical joints and improve the strength of the brick post.

3 **Tap the bricks** into place with the brick trowel. It is best to "butter" the ends of the bricks with mortar as you lay them, because this will fill the joints between the bricks as they are laid. Fill any gaps around the post with mortar.

4 Stagger the joints as you lay more courses, checking the post is square and that the courses are level. Clean away any excess mortar.

HOW IT WORKS

Each wooden post is securely bedded in a footing of hardcore (crushed stones) topped with concrete. At ground level, the post is then surrounded by mortared bricks to the desired height. It is a solid construction, perfect for substantial pergolas clothed with heavy plants.

5 Continue to your desired height and finish with a layer of coping (*see below*). Tidy up the mortar in the joints with a pointing trowel; when it is dry, smooth over with a stiff brush.

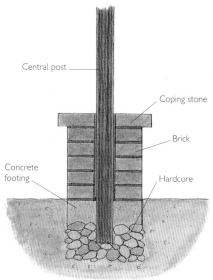

Central post

Coping stone

Brick

Concrete footing

Hardcore

FINISHING OFF

You may wish to cap your brick posts (this has the added benefit of keeping water out of the posts). Either use more bricks laid on their sides or a decorative layer of coping stones; there are many materials other than brick from which to choose. Tiles in terracotta or good imitations in concrete make an excellent hardwearing coping, which links well with terraces built in the same material. Natural or reconstituted stone slabs can be cut and laid around a pergola post as suitable coping stones. Sandstone is also ideal; it is durable and warm in colour – ideal for a garden setting.

STONE

TERRACOTTA

SANDSTONE

BACK TO BASICS

PRACTICAL MATTERS

THE SECRET OF A SUCCESSFUL ARCH or pergola lies not only in a carefully planned design, but also in sound construction. A well-made arch or pergola will look impressive and remain solid for many years if you do not cut corners. Always use good quality tools and the right materials, and set aside enough time to do the job properly. You should be able to do most construction work yourself, although you may wish to employ a bricklayer to build brick posts.

TOOLS REQUIRED

If you plan to carry out much construction work, it is worth investing in your own set of good quality tools. The tasks of setting out, groundwork, woodwork, and brickwork require a particular assortment of equipment. If you are planning only one project, then consider hiring equipment. Most tool hire shops will carry the items required for the projects in this book. Make sure you have what you need before you start: stopping or improvising half-way through is inconvenient and even dangerous.

PLANNING PERMISSION

• Before building an overhead structure, check possible restrictions with your local authority.

• Height restrictions may apply to structures along the boundary of your property. Structures well within your garden are less likely to need planning permission.

• If you live within a conservation area, or your property is a protected building, the planners may need to be satisfied that the proposed structure is in keeping with the locality or architecture.

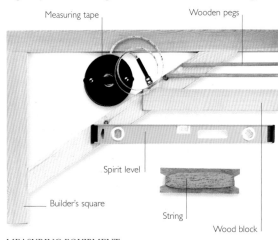

Measuring tape

Wooden pegs

Spirit level

Builder's square

String

Wood block

MEASURING EQUIPMENT
Accurate measurements are crucial to the success of your structure. Shown here is a basic measuring kit.

MARKING OUT THE SITE

A good design will be spoilt by inaccurate setting out. Avoid the temptation to rush ahead, but take your time when measuring to make sure, first of all, that everything is square. Do not guesstimate the position of post holes, but use a builder's square, string line, and wooden pegs to guarantee accuracy. Be consistent with which side of the pegs you measure from: inside to inside or outside to outside. Always double-check measurements before starting to dig or cutting lengths of timber.

PLANNING TIPS

• Check the diagonal measurements between corners to confirm post positions are correct.
• Allow at least 2.1m (7ft) head clearance between ground level and the underside of the overhead beams.
• Posts for taller pergolas should be a minimum of 10x10cm (4x4in) thick.
• Overhead cross-beams are usually about 15x5cm (6x2in) thick, with rafters of the same measurement or 10x5cm (4x2in).

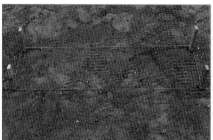

1 **Mark two post** positions, front and back on one side, with timber pegs, builder's square, and string. Then, using the square and string, mark the position of the other two posts.

2 **Once all four points** have been set, check all the base measurements including the diagonals (which should be identical lengths) to confirm that everything is correctly set out.

MEASURING ACCURATELY

As work progresses, develop the habit of checking measurements regularly with a steel tape and frequently confirm that posts are vertical and beams are horizontal, using a spirit level. Avoid approximating or guessing measurements and always double-check them before cutting out joints or permanently fixing with screws or nails.

MEASURING RAFTERS
Rafters should be spaced out evenly on the overhead beams. Mark all the positions on both beams with a pencil. This is especially important if you are cutting notches yourself.

VERTICAL CHECK
Use a spirit level on the front and side of each spiked metal post support to check that they are driven into the ground vertically.

RAW MATERIALS

IF YOU ARE BUILDING AN ARCH or pergola from scratch as opposed to buying one in kit form, then it will help to familiarize yourself with the basic construction materials. Most building supply stores have displays that are well set out, clear sales literature, and expert advice readily on hand, which means that you should soon gain sufficient knowledge of the various products and quantities required for you to get started.

CONCRETE AND MORTAR

Most large custom-built arches or pergolas need a footing to hold posts firm, or as the foundation for bricks. These are formed from a layer of hardcore topped with concrete – a mix of aggregate (mixed grades of gravel), cement, and water. The mortar used between bricks is a mix of sand, cement, and water. You can prepare both concrete and mortar yourself (*see below*) or buy ready-prepared mixes from a supplier.

SAND

DRY MORTAR

CEMENT

WET MORTAR MIX

QUANTITIES AND MIXING

Until you gain some experience, it is easy to under or over estimate amounts; ask suppliers for advice. Concrete for footings is often a mix of one part cement to six parts aggregate mixed with water. Mortar for brickwork is one part cement to five or six parts builder's sand, mixed with water and plasticizer (an additive to make mortar easier to work).

SUPPLIERS

• Large building suppliers display detailed information to help you choose materials.
• For small projects, buy small pre-packed mixes of concrete and mortar.
• Ask for kits, and heavy, bulky construction material to be delivered to your door.

KNOW YOUR QUANTITIES
To make mortar, a 25kg (55lb) bag of sand will need about 5kg of cement. Allow an area of at least 1m (3ft) square for mixing.

CHOOSING TIMBER

Hardwoods may be used for construction, but they are expensive and more difficult to work with than softwood, which is most commonly used. Softwood for garden structures is supplied already pressure-treated with preservative. It may be bought as sawn timber, which does not have a planed finish, or planed all around. Planed timber is more expensive, but more suitable if you wish to paint or stain your pergola.

MAKING NOTCHES

Rafters that are notched and nailed onto overhead beams not only give a stronger fixing, but also look more pleasing than ones that have simply been nailed into place. A T-joint joins two pieces of wood at right angles to one another. A half-lap joint is similar, but at least one notch is at the end of the wood. A sturdy and streamlined effect can be gained by cutting a notch in both the beam and rafter so that they fit flush in a halving joint. To make a joint, cut each side of the notch with a saw to the desired depth and make a series of saw cuts in the area of the joint to that same depth. Carefully chisel out the notch with a mallet and sharp wood chisel.

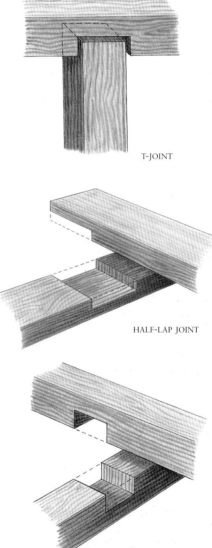

T-JOINT

HALF-LAP JOINT

HALVING JOINT

CHISELLING OUT A JOINT
Measure and mark where your joint should be. Make saw cuts at either end of the notch and then use a mallet and a sharp wood chisel to carefully cut out the notch.

SAFETY AND MAINTENANCE

GREAT CARE MUST BE TAKEN when working outside to protect yourself and others. Always work in a safe manner, using the right tools for the right job. Tools should be well maintained in a good condition. Familiarize yourself with rented equipment, especially power tools, and ask for a demonstration before using them yourself. Pay attention to the maintenance of your arch, pergola or arbour to ensure your own safety and that of other people.

WORKING SAFELY

Safe working practice means far more than, for example, not using electrical equipment in the rain. It begins with what you wear and means applying common sense to every operation that you carry out. Make sure you keep warm and dry, and wear the correct protective clothing such as sturdy footwear, gloves when using cement, and goggles and ear protectors when using a power saw. Plan the work carefully and do not set yourself unrealistic targets, which all too easily lead to tiredness, errors, and accidents. All the projects in this book are best carried out by at least two people; always ask for help when lifting heavy or awkward loads such as cross-beams, and try to avoid balancing and stretching at the top of ladders.

USING A DRIVING TOOL
Knocking in a spiked post support with a driving tool avoids damaging the metal, which would give a nasty jagged edge and make it far more difficult to fit the post. A piece of wood as a buffer will work just as well.

HAMMERING WITH BUFFER
Where possible, use an offcut of wood as a buffer between the hammer and a notched rafter when knocking it into place. It protects the rafter from splitting and splintering, and prevents the hammer head leaving marks on softwood.

SAFETY TIPS

• Wear suitable clothing and use safety equipment.
• Tie up long hair and avoid loose clothing when working with machinery.
• Set yourself realistic targets to avoid tiredness, errors, and accidents.
• Work comfortably, not stretching or balancing.
• Saw wood and cut joints on firm ground, ideally using a work bench.
• Ensure ladders are properly locked into position and secured firmly before using.
• Always chisel wood away from, never towards, yourself.
• Fit circuit breakers when using electric equipment.
• Use cordless drills in preference to electric drills with cables.
• Do not use electric equipment in wet conditions.

PAINTING AND STAINING

Plastic-coated metal needs no painting, but other metals should be sealed to prevent rust. Hardwoods, and some softwoods such as cedar, which has its own protective resin, require no additional treatment. Most softwoods, however, need protection when used in outdoor constructions, and are normally sold having already been pressure-treated with preservative. As well as offering some extra protection, stains on treated wood give a desired colour effect. Untreated timber can be stained or painted both for protection and colour. Painting can be fairly laborious, as several coats are required; staining requires only two coats. Stains are easier to apply and are available in a wide range of colours. Where possible, paint or stain, and allow the treatment to dry thoroughly before planting.

MAINTENANCE TIPS

• Protect timber with preservative on a regular basis to maintain its condition.
• Improve the appearance of old wood arches and pergolas by applying a coloured stain.
• Mend rotten posts by bolting on a concrete spur, which is in turn set in the ground.
• Firm up loose posts by setting concrete around the base.
• Check bolts and nail fixings frequently and replace if necessary.
• Sand down old timber to remove splinters.
• Oil hardwoods to keep them in pristine condition, or allow them to weather naturally.
• Tie back climbing plants and cover ground-level plants when sanding or staining posts.
• Treat metal structures for rust and paint with a rustproof paint.
• Avoid windy days for painting and staining.

STAINING TIMBER
Applying stain to planed timber, here an arbour seat, is a far quicker job than painting, requiring fewer coats. A wide range of wood tones and soft or bright colours is available.

APPLYING PRESERVATIVE
Trellis is often pre-treated with preservative. If you are applying it yourself, wear protective gloves as some preservatives are difficult to wash off and can also cause skin irritation.

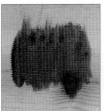

RUST-RED

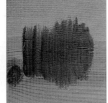

SAGE-GREEN

YELLOW OCHRE

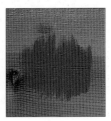

RICH BLUE

CLOTHING THE STRUCTURE

CLIMBING PLANTS ARE CHOSEN FOR THEIR SUITABILITY to clothe a pergola so that it remains as an open structure: if they are too rampant, the form of the framework is lost, and can spoil the effect. A single climber may be the most effective way to cover a pergola: too many climbers all vying for attention may produce an unsatisfactory result. Whatever you choose, note its pruning and other requirements to ensure that it suits the site and gives you the best display.

SUPPORTING YOUR PLANTS

All climbers need a helping hand early on, to twine around pergola posts and scramble over beams. Encourage your plants to climb by securing vertical wires onto the posts and attaching horizontal wires to the cross-beams and rafters. Tie the shoots to these, releasing them and re-tying as the stems thicken, if necessary. Greater coverage will be achieved if wires are also stretched between the rafters or, for a shadehouse effect, fix trellis or slatted timber battens across the top of the pergola. Allow the plants to grow straight up the wires to reach the top of the pergola quickly or, if you prefer the posts to be generously covered, let them bush out by twining the plants around each post and tying them in. Bare stems at the bottom of posts can be filled in by annual climbers.

Twine climbers around posts for maximum cover

Keep flowering shoots in check to maintain the form of the pergola

Quick-growing annuals, such as morning glory (*Ipomoea*) will cover the bare stems of vigorous climbers

PRUNING TIPS

• Check the plant label or a reference book to determine the exact pruning requirements of each climber.
• Take care that you prune at the right time of the year to encourage flowers. Getting it wrong may mean the loss of flowers for a whole season.
• Some climbers need light pruning after flowering, others need hard pruning to encourage new growth.
• Prune vigorous climbers regularly to keep them in check; aim to maintain the structure's shape and to allow good access.
• Use secateurs and long-handled pruners on new growth and a pruning saw on old, thick wood.

PLANTING DISTANCES
Plant the climber a short distance away from the post to give the roots space. Pull back and tie in the stems.

STRAINING WIRES
Run plastic-coated, galvanized wires through hoops on the posts and beams, then train the climbers onto them.

TYING IN
Tie the stems onto the wires with soft twine; be careful not to damage them. Re-tie as they grow, if necessary.

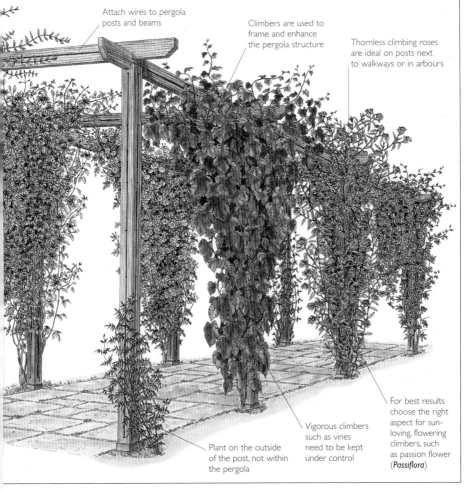

Attach wires to pergola posts and beams

Climbers are used to frame and enhance the pergola structure

Thornless climbing roses are ideal on posts next to walkways or in arbours

For best results choose the right aspect for sun-loving, flowering climbers, such as passion flower (*Passiflora*)

Vigorous climbers such as vines need to be kept under control

Plant on the outside of the post, not within the pergola

INDEX

ACKNOWLEDGMENTS

Picture research Cathie Arrington

Special photography Peter Anderson; also Steve Gorton, Jacqui Hurst, Dave King, and Tim Ridley

Illustrations Karen Gavin

Index Hilary Bird

Dorling Kindersley would like to thank:
Simon Maughan for editorial assistance; Murdo Culver for his practical skills; Neale Chamberlain for sourcing pictures from the DK library; Agriframes for donating the metal arch featured on pp.36–39; and all staff at the Royal Horticultural Society, in particular Susanne Mitchell, Karen Wilson, and Barbara Haynes at Vincent Square.

The Royal Horticultural Society
To learn more about the work of the society, visit the RHS on the Internet at www.rhs.org.uk. Information includes news of events around the country, a horticultural database, international plant registers, results of plant trials, and membership details.

Cover photograhy: commissioned photography except front: Garden Matters lc below, Photos Horticultural r; back: Gerry Harpur tr, Clive Nichols b, Harry Smith tl

Photography
The publisher would also like to thank the following for their kind permission to reproduce their photographs:
(key: t=top, b=bottom, l=left, r=right, c=centre)

Bridgeman Art Library: (from Roman de la Rose, c. 1487–95, British Library Harl.4425.f.12v) 7c
Garden Matters: 4br; 14; 15t; 20bl
Garden Picture Library: John Baker 52; Philippe Bonduel 8; Tommy Candler 23b; Ron Evans 40; Nigel Francis 24r; Sunniva Harte 28r; Roger Hyam 23t, 48; Zara McCalmont 9t; John Miller 58; Jerry Pavia 30r; Joanne Pavia 44; Clay Perry 32; Howard Rice 19b; Steven Wooster 6, 33
John Glover Photography: 2; 17t; 26r
Harpur Garden Library: Jonathan Baillie, London 10t, Designer Bruce Kelly, New York 15b; 23t; 29t
Andrew Lawson: 11
Clive Nichols: Designer Elizabeth Woodhouse 5br, 36; Designer Paula Rainey Crofts 10b; Sleightholme Dale, Yorkshire 19t; The Old Rectory, Farnborough 20br; Vale End, Surrey 21b
Photos Horticultural: 9b; Designer Julian Dowle 16; 17b; 18; 22
Harry Smith Collection: 4bl; 12; 13b; 29b; 56b